*kimmy*

W9-BYT-684

# Table of Contents

## STEP ONE: NOUNS, PRONOUNS, AND VERBS

Nouns - nouns ................................. **1**
Reviewing Nouns - nouns .................... **2**
Proper Nouns - nouns ........................ **3**
Plurals - nouns ............................. **4**
Singular and Plural Nouns - nouns ............. **5**
Plural Nouns - nouns ....................... **6**
Forming Plurals - nouns .................... **7**
More Plurals - nouns ...................... **8**
Plurals - nouns ........................... **9**
Reviewing Plurals - nouns ................. **10**
Collective Nouns - nouns ................. **11**
Collective Nouns - nouns ................. **12**
Pronouns - pronouns ...................... **13**
Subject Pronouns - pronouns .............. **14**
Pronouns - pronouns ...................... **15**
Object Pronouns - pronouns ............... **16**
Object Pronouns - pronouns ............... **17**
Possessive Pronouns - pronouns ........... **18**
Possessive Pronouns - pronouns ........... **19**
Verbs - verbs ............................. **20**
Present Tense - verbs ..................... **21**
Past Tense of Regular Verbs - verbs ....... **22**
Past Tense - verbs ........................ **23**
Other Forms of Active Verbs - verbs ....... **24**
Future Tense - verbs ...................... **25**
BE Words - verbs .......................... **26**
The Verb BE - verbs ....................... **27**
The ING Verb Form - verbs ................. **28**
Unscrambling Sentences - verbs ............ **29**
First and Third Person Verbs - verbs ...... **30**
Making Questions - verbs .................. **31**
Noun or Verb? - nouns and verbs ........... **32**
Same Word - Different Use - nouns and verbs ...... **33**

## STEP TWO: DESCRIBING WORDS

Adjectives - adjectives ................... **34**
Adjectives - adjectives ................... **35**
Adjectives - adjectives ................... **36**
Adjectives - adjectives ................... **37**
More Adjectives - adjectives .............. **38**
Predicate Adjectives - adjectives ......... **39**
Adjectives and Predicate Adjectives - adjectives ... **40**
Adverbs - adverbs ......................... **41**
Adverbs - adverbs ......................... **42**

**continued on next page**

©1983, Instructional Fair, Inc.

continued from previous page

**More Adverbs** - adverbs ...................... **43**
**Adjectives and Adverbs** - adjectives/adverbs ....... **44**
**Using Prepositions** - prepositions ............... **45**
**Prepositions** - prepositions ................... **46**
**Reviewing Prepositions** - prepositions ........... **47**
**Finding Prepositions and Their Nouns** - prepositions . **48**
**Prepositional Phrases** - prepositions ............. **49**
**Prepositional Phrases** - prepositions ............. **50**

**STEP THREE: PARTS OF SPEECH AND SENTENCES**
**Parts of Speech** - parts of speech .............. **51**
**Scrambled Sentences** - parts of speech .......... **52**
**Classifying Words** - parts of speech ............. **53**
**Compound Subjects** - parts of speech ........... **54**
**Making Sentences** - sentences ................. **55**
**Two Parts of a Sentence** - subjects and predicates .. **56**
**Sentence Parts** - subjects and predicates ......... **57**
**Subject and Predicate** - subjects and predicates .... **58**
**Subject and Predicate** - subjects and predicates .... **59**

**STEP FOUR: LANGUAGE SKILLS**
**First Word in a Sentence** - capitalization ........ **60**
**Capitals and Quotations** - capitalization .......... **61**
**Proper Nouns** - capitalization .................. **62**
**Names, Titles, and "I"** - capitalization ........... **63**
**Names of Groups** - capitalization ............... **64**
**Groups and Languages** - capitalization ........... **65**
**Historical Terms** - capitalization ................ **66**
**Geographic Names** - capitalization .............. **67**
**Directional Terms** - capitalization .............. **68**
**Titles** - capitalization ....................... **69**
**Names of Time Periods** - capitalization .......... **70**
**Capitalizing in Sentences** - capitalization ........ **71**
**Capitals in Poetry** - capitalization .............. **72**
**Telling and Commanding Sentences** - punctuation .. **73**
**Questions** - punctuation ...................... **74**
**Exclamatory Sentences** - punctuation ........... **75**
**City and State** - punctuation ................... **76**
**Day of Month and Year** - punctuation ........... **77**
**Greetings and Closings** - punctuation ........... **78**
**Punctuating Sentences** - punctuation ........... **79**
**Abbreviations** - abbreviations .................. **80**
**Abbreviations** - abbreviations .................. **81**
**Abbreviations** - abbreviations .................. **82**
**Initials** - abbreviations ...................... **83**
**Using the Dictionary** - dictionary usage .......... **84**
**Dictionary Usage** - dictionary usage ............. **85**
**Using the Dictionary** - dictionary usage .......... **86**

©1983, Instructional Fair, Inc.

# Nouns

**<u>noun</u>: a word that is used to name any person, place, or thing.**

As you read the following sentences, circle all of the nouns. The number in parentheses at the end of each sentence tells you how many nouns are in that sentence.

Ex. The (teacher) asked her (pupils) to open their (books). (3)

1. (Grocers) sell (meats,) (vegetables) (fruit,) (breads,) (pastries,) (drinks,) (soaps,) and many other (kinds) of (things). (10)

2. The (table) and the (chair) had put marks on the new (tile) on the (floor). (5)

3. (Gather) scissors, (tape,) (paper,) (pencils,) (crayons,) and (string) for this (project). (7)

4. The (kite) would not fly because there was not enough (wind) and the (tail) was too short. (3)

5. The (police) arrested three (suspects) and confiscated three stolen (watches) hidden in the (glove) compartment of their (car). (5)

6. The (cocoa) was so hot that the (little boy) dropped his (cup,) because he had burned his (mouth). (4)

7. My (desk) is covered with so much (junk) that you cannot even see the (top). (3)

**The Rule**

Nouns, Pronouns, and Verbs

# Begin Step 1

**1**

# Reviewing Nouns

**The Rule**   Nouns are words that name people, objects and places. Underline the subject noun in the sentences below.

1. Jimmy played baseball this morning.

2. My sister rode her bicycle to the store.

3. Mrs. Garcia has just gone to the market.

4. At school the swings were quite popular.

5. Tess is singing too loudly.

6. Those people are buying a new boat.

These sentences have a subject noun and a noun after the verb. Underline the two nouns.

7. Carlos was playing with his brother.

8. The tomatoes are in a basket.

9. The new girl's name is Sara.

10. The apples fell from the tree.

11. That store carries many supplies.

12. Bill is going to Florida.

**2**

# Proper Nouns

Proper nouns name special people, places and things, and begin with a **The Rule** capital letter. Rewrite the sentences. Capitalize the proper nouns.

1. The capital of iowa is des moines.

   _The capital of Iowa is Des Moines._

2. Please give the package to joan or tim.

   _Please give the packag to Ioan or Tim._

3. Both lou and i will go to clausen's store.

   _Both Lou and I will go to Clausen's Store._

4. mr. taylor is ronnie's new teacher.

   _Mr. taylor is Ronnie's new teacher._

5. The queen of england lives in windsor castle.

   _The Queen of England lives in Windsor Castle._

6. The hudson river is in the state of new york.

   _The Hudso rizer is the State of N. Y_

7. Marshal field and co. is a store in chicago.

   _Marshal Field and CO. is a store in Chicago._

**3**

# **Plurals**

Change the noun on the left from singular to plural. Write the plural noun on the line.

tooth  1. My ___teeth___ are going to be cleaned today.

child  2. The ___children___ will see a magic show.

party  3. Halloween ___partys___ were held in every room.

man  4. Four ___men___ were going to sing at the party.

sheep  5. Mr. Tan's ___sheeps___ are out in the field.

daisy  6. The ___daisys___ were planted in the rock garden.

turkey  7. The ___turkeys___ in that flock are all white.

foot  8. My ___feet___ hurt after the long walk.

mouse  9. The ___meuse___ got into the house and made a mess.

school  10. The ___school___ were closed for two weeks.

**4**

# Singular and Plural Nouns

The plurals of most nouns are formed by adding **s**. The plurals of **The Rule** most remaining nouns are formed by these rules.

1. Add **s** to nouns ending in a vowel + **y**.
2. Add **es** to nouns ending in **s**, **x**, **z**, **ch**, and **sh**.
3. Change the **y** to **i** and add **es** to nouns ending with a consonant + **y**.

## Write the plurals of these words.

1. band _bands_     9. mouth _mouths_

2. day _days_     10. class _classes_

3. address _addresses_   11. cry _cryies_

4. lady _ladies_   12. push _____

5. drum _drumes_   13. flag _flags_

6. catch _catchs_   14. pony _ponies_

7. press _presses_   15. sea _seas_

8. country _countries_   16. mess _messes_

**5**

# **Plural Nouns**

**The Rule** To make nouns that end in <u>o</u> plural add <u>s</u> or <u>es</u>. Match these singular and plural nouns.

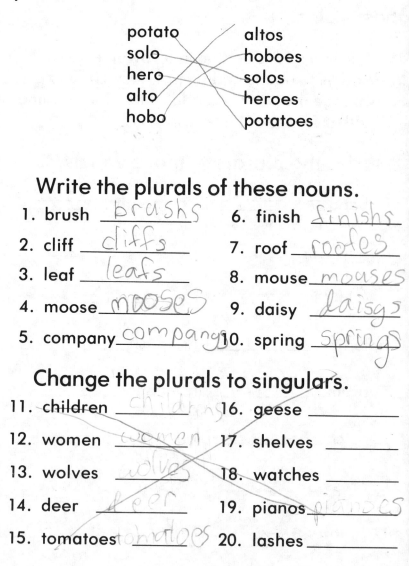

potato     altos
solo     hoboes
hero     solos
alto     heroes
hobo     potatoes

## Write the plurals of these nouns.

1. brush _brushs_
2. cliff _cliffs_
3. leaf _leafs_
4. moose _mooses_
5. company _companys_

6. finish _finishs_
7. roof _roofes_
8. mouse _mouses_
9. daisy _daisys_
10. spring _springs_

## Change the plurals to singulars.

11. children _childring_
12. women _women_
13. wolves _wolves_
14. deer _deer_
15. tomatoes _tomatoes_

16. geese _____
17. shelves _____
18. watches _____
19. pianos _pianoes_
20. lashes _____

**6**

# Forming Plurals

## Read the words in the box.

| yourselves | puppies | sheep | wives |
|---|---|---|---|
| enemies | shelves | women | groceries |

Write both singular and plural forms for those spelling words whose singular form ends with the /**f**/ sound.

| Singular | Plural |
|---|---|
| 1. __lotfother__ | __fethers__ |
| 2. _____ | _____ |
| 3. _____ | _____ |

Write the words whose singular form ends in **y**.

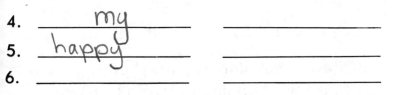

| 4. __my__ | _____ |
| 5. __happy__ | _____ |
| 6. _____ | _____ |

Write the word whose spelling remains the same.

7. _____     _____

Write the word whose spelling changes within the word.

8. _____     _____

**7**

# More Plurals

## Read the words in the box.

| | | | | |
|---|---|---|---|---|
| beliefs | knives | geese | selves | wolves |
| mice | roofs | teeth | leaves | chiefs |

1. Write the plurals of these words.

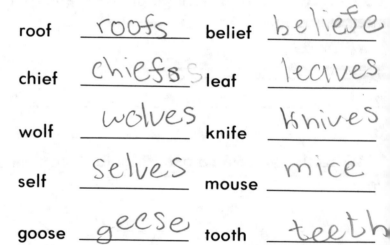

roof _roofs_    belief _beliefe_

chief _chiefss_    leaf _leaves_

wolf _wolves_    knife _knives_

self _selves_    mouse _mice_

goose _geese_    tooth _teeth_

2. Write the spelling words that are plurals formed by changing the word from within.

_teeth_ _geese_ _mice_

3. Write the spelling words that are plurals formed by changing the **f** to **v** and adding **es**.

_____ _____

_____ _____

**8**

# Plurals

---

Read the words in the box.

| | | | |
|---|---|---|---|
| bodies | monkeys | masses | latches |
| pennies | losses | turkeys | libraries |
| | countries | coaches | |

1.  Write the plurals of these words.

    monkey _____     turkey _____

    mass _____     coach _____

    loss _____     latch _____

    country_____     body _____

    penny _____     library _____

2.  Add **s** to make a plural when a vowel is before the letter _____.

3.  Add **es** to make a plural when the ending of the singular word is **ss** or _____.

4.  Change _____ to _____ and add **es** when an ending **y** has a consonant before it.

**9**

# Reviewing Plurals

Write the singular form of these plural nouns. Then write the number of the rule that tells how the plural was formed:

**The Rule**

1.) Add <u>s</u>.
2.) Add <u>es</u> if the word ends in <u>ch</u> or <u>sh</u>.
3.) Change the <u>y</u> to <u>i</u> and add <u>es</u>.
4.) Change the <u>f</u> to <u>v</u> and add <u>es</u>.
5.) Change letters of the word.
6.) Leave the word the same.

## The first one is done for you.

| 1. houses | house | 1 |
|---|---|---|
| 2. berries | _____ | _____ |
| 3. children | _____ | _____ |
| 4. matches | _____ | _____ |
| 5. knives | _____ | _____ |
| 6. mice | _____ | _____ |
| 7. apples | _____ | _____ |
| 8. fish | _____ | _____ |
| 9. geese | _____ | _____ |
| 10. crashes | _____ | _____ |
| 11. puppies | _____ | _____ |

**10**

# Collective Nouns

The Rule

Collective nouns are not the same thing as plurals. A collective noun is a noun that represents a large group, and the group is thought of as a singular item. A plural noun is a noun that represents a large group, but the group is considered a collection of individuals.

A collective noun is used with a singular verb:    The class is ready.

A plural noun is used with a plural verb:    The children are ready.

Underline the noun in each sentence. Circle the correct verb in each sentence. Write collective or plural at the end of each sentence.

Ex. The  <u>children</u>  (is, (are))
doing the work.         plural

1.  The troop (is, are) leaving tomorrow.  _____

2.  The crowd (is, are) moving toward the door.  _____

3.  The committee (is, are) meeting down the hall.  _____

4.  The men (is, are) having a conference.  _____

**11**

  ©1983, Instructional Fair, Inc.

# Collective Nouns

**The Rule** <u>collective</u> <u>noun</u>: a noun which names a group:

## <u>crowd</u> - <u>team</u> - <u>class</u>

Collective nouns stand for many people, objects, or things but they are treated as one thing.

Circle the collective noun in each sentence.

Ex. The (crowd) wants the game to begin.

1. The audience loves the circus.

2. The navy wears blue uniforms.

3. Our army wears olive drab uniforms.

4. The committee meets on Thursday.

5. That swarm stays near the old hive.

6. The government is working on the problem.

7. The team has the best average.

8. This group is larger than that group.

9. The club plans to have a party a week from Thursday.

10. The church is planning a picnic.

**12**

# Pronouns

Use the subject pronouns <u>it</u>, <u>he</u>, <u>she</u>, <u>we</u>, or <u>they</u> in place of the underlined subjects. Write the pronoun you use on the line.

1. <u>The boat</u> is on the water. _____

2. <u>Roy</u> will leave tomorrow. _____

3. <u>Dot</u> is the leader this week. _____

4. <u>Lin and Lisa</u> are the readers. _____

5. <u>My friend and I</u> will both go. _____

6. <u>The boys</u> are playing a game. _____

7. <u>An apple</u> is a kind of fruit. _____

8. <u>Dr. Edna Gates</u> is my doctor. _____

9. <u>Bob and Bea</u> are twins. _____

10. <u>The new pet</u> is a lively puppy. _____

11. <u>Mr. White</u> whittles wood. _____

12. <u>Robins and sparrows</u> are birds. _____

**13**

# Subject Pronouns

Fill in the blank spaces in the chart below with words from the box.

| woman | girl | it | he |
|-------|------|-----|-----|
| Fluffy | Dr. Ford | we | Carl |
| Ella | boys | they | she |

|  | Common noun | Proper Noun | Pronoun |
|----|-------------|-------------|---------|
| 1. | cat | | |
| 2. | | | she |
| 3. | | Ken and Matt | |
| 4. | uncle | | |
| 5. | dentist | | |
| 6. | | Mrs. Brown | |

Write a pronoun in place of each subject in the sentences.

7. My cat (_____) purrs loudly.

8. Two boys (_____) are having a swimming lesson.

9. Our doctor (_____) is a fine worker.

**14**

# Pronouns

On the line write the object pronoun that could be used in place of each underlined noun or pronoun. The object pronouns are: <u>me</u>, <u>you</u>, <u>it</u>, <u>him</u>, <u>her</u>, <u>us</u>, <u>them</u>. The first one is done for you.

1. Give the book to <u>father</u>. ___him___

2. Becky was carrying the <u>apples</u>.
   _____

3. Pam could not find the <u>policeman</u>.
   _____

4. The gift is for <u>Dot</u> and <u>me</u>. _____

5. Please feed the <u>dog</u>. _____

6. "I need some help. Please help _____ ."

7. Eric rang the <u>school bell</u>. _____

8. "Here, John, this is for _____."

9. Mother will take <u>Riki</u> and <u>me</u>. _____

10. The prize is for the <u>girls</u>. _____

11. Bring the toy to the <u>kitten</u>. _____

12. "There, Mother, I made this for _____."

## 15

# Object Pronouns

**The Rule**    Object pronouns (<u>me</u>, <u>you</u>, <u>it</u>, <u>him</u>, <u>her</u>, <u>us</u> and <u>them</u>) may be used after prepositions. The subject form is at the left of each sentence. Write the object form after the preposition.

we     1. Give that sled to _____.

they    2. That package came from
          _____.

she     3. I went to the show with _____.

he      4. The picture was made by _____.

I        5. Please give the card to _____.

it       6. We must make _____
          carefully.

we     7. The gift is from both of _____.

he,    8. The two pieces of cake can be given to
she          _____ and _____.

they    9. The rock seemed to be aimed at
          _____.

I       10. Will you come after _____?

## 16

# Object Pronouns

Object pronouns are <u>me</u>, <u>you</u>, <u>it</u>, <u>him</u>, <u>her</u>, <u>us</u> and <u>them</u>. Replace the object noun in each sentence with an object pronoun. The first one is done for you.

1. Can you do the exercises (_____them_____) ?

2. Would you like to play the piano (_____)?

3. I will tell Susan ( _____ ) the secret.

4. The committee awarded the prize (_____) to several children.

5. The door bumped Edna and me (_____).

6. Give the paper to John (_____).

7. Can we spend the money (_____) now?

8. My school will provide everyone (_____) with books.

9. Please help Dean and Roy (_____) gather the newspapers.

**17**

# Possessive Pronouns

**The Rule** <u>possessive</u> <u>pronoun</u>: a pronoun which shows ownership:

<u>our</u> - <u>yours</u> - <u>his</u> - <u>theirs</u> - <u>my</u> - <u>mine</u>

All of the following sentences have used possessive pronouns correctly.

1. This is <u>my</u> book. This book is <u>mine</u>. This one is <u>mine</u>. This is <u>mine</u>.

2. This is <u>your</u> ball. This ball is <u>yours</u>. This one is <u>yours</u>. This is <u>yours</u>.

3. This is <u>its</u> nest. This nest is <u>its</u>. This one is <u>its</u>. This is <u>its</u>.

4. This is <u>his</u> tree. This tree is <u>his</u>. This one is <u>his</u>. This is <u>his</u>.

5. This is <u>their</u> home. This house is <u>theirs</u>. This one is <u>theirs</u>. This is <u>theirs</u>.

Which pronouns were used as an adjective before a noun? _____

_____

Which pronouns can be used instead of a noun?_____

_____

Which pronouns can be used both with a noun and alone? _____

## 18

# Possessive Pronouns

**possessive** **pronoun:** a pronoun which shows ownership:

**hers - their - ours - his - her - your**

**(No pronoun ever has an apostrophe.)**

Cross out the word just before the blank in each sentence. Write the pronoun that should have been used instead of the word that was used.

Ex. Is this ~~you~~ __your__ book?

1. Where are me _____ shoes?

2. The dog is our's _____ .

3. Is that they're _____ cat?

4. Do not play with he _____ toys.

5. Me _____ foot hurts.

6. Ours _____ house is green.

7. Which one is your's _____ ?

**19**

# Verbs

**verb: a word used to tell about actions.**

**The Rule** Circle the action word in each of the following sentences.

Ex. We (vacuumed) the carpet.

1. Birds build nests in the spring.

2. This product scrubs best.

3. We plant gardens in the spring.

4. It rains every evening here.

5. We bought a new car.

6. Our baseball team practices twice a week during baseball season.

7. They fished all day.

8. He shoveled all the snow away.

9. They ice-skate very well.

10. We rode our bicycles into town.

11. Jerry bought a new shirt.

12. We raked all of the leaves.

13. The dog barked all night.

14. Jan baked a cake.

15. The Clarks painted their house.

The Homework Booklet ©1983, Instructional Fair, Inc.

# Present Tense

Most verbs end in <u>s</u> when used with the pronouns <u>he</u>, <u>she</u>, or <u>it</u>. Rewrite the sentences below using the pronoun given as the subject and the <u>s</u> form of the verb.  **The Rule**

1. The children swim in the pool.

(he) _____

2. The girls bake cookies on Monday.

(she) _____

3. Snakes crawl in the grass.

(it) _____

4. I like chocolate cake.

(he) _____

5. We plant flowers in the spring.

(she) _____

6. Ned and I enjoy helping at the zoo.

(he) _____

**21**

# Past Tense of Regular Verbs

**The Rule**    Add <u>d</u> or <u>ed</u> to form the past tense of most regular verbs. For other regular verbs, follow these rules:

1.) If a word ends with a <u>consonant</u> + <u>y</u>, change the <u>y</u> to <u>i</u> and add <u>ed</u>. (worry - worried)

2.) If the word ends with a <u>vowel</u> + <u>consonant</u>, double the consonant and add <u>ed</u>. (stop - stopped)

Write the past tense of these verbs.

1. sort _____    9. worry_____

2. cry _____    10. carry _____

3. close _____    11. sip _____

4. burn _____    12. beg _____

5. dare _____    13. like _____

6. fry _____    14. bake _____

7. push _____    15. spy_____

8. cross _____    16. stop _____

## 22

# Past Tense

Some past tense verbs have a helping verb. Cross out the incorrect verb form and underline the complete verb. The first one is done for you.

1. Our lunch (~~will~~, <u>has</u>) <u>turned</u> cold.

2. The log jam in the river (had, have) moved downstream.

3. The trails (has, have) become dusty.

4. The boys (were, was) skating on the pond.

5. We (have, has) gone to the zoo before.

6. The children (were, has) eating ice cream when the rain came.

7. My neighbor (have, has) planted all his rose bushes.

8. We can't come for dinner since we (have, were) already eaten.

9. The weather (has, was) remained the same all week.

10. The policeman (was, will) listening to the radio.

**23**

# Other Forms of Active Verbs

**The Rule**   Active verbs add <u>d</u> or <u>ed</u> to show what happened in the past. In the blank space write the past form of the verb shown on the left. The first one is done for you.

visit   1. Lee ___visited___ his Grandmother.

hunt   2. Dad and I _____ for squirrels.

climb   3. Joe _____ the big tree in his backyard.

close   4. Our school _____ early today.

pick   5. Henry _____ the ripe apples.

cheer   6. The crowd _____ when the team won the game.

taste   7. The bread _____ good.

plant   8. We _____ a garden last year.

wash   9. Father and Pam _____ the truck.

pull   10. The dogs _____ the sled through the snow.

# 24

# Future Tense

**Tense means time.**

**future tense: verbs used to express action that will occur at some time in the future.**

*The Rule*

**Future tense is formed with will and shall.**

Underline the first verb in each sentence. Fill each blank with the future tense of the underlined verb.

Ex. I <u>work</u> here; I _____ here tomorrow.     <u>shall work</u>

1. We plant a garden; we _____ a garden tomorrow.     _____

2. We bake bread; we _____ bread tomorrow.     _____

3. We can vegetables; we _____ tomorrow.     _____

4. He waters the plants; he _____ the plants tomorrow.     _____

**25**

# BE Words

**The Rule**    <u>Am</u>, <u>is</u>, <u>are</u>, <u>was</u> and <u>were</u> are used with active verbs that end in <u>ing</u>. Underline the <u>be</u> verb in each sentence. Then change the verb on the left by adding <u>ing</u>. If the word ends in <u>e</u> drop the <u>e</u> before adding <u>ing</u>. The first one is done for you.

| | |
|---|---|
| dance | 1. The children <u>were</u> _____dancing_____ at noon. |

sing    2. A happy group was _____.

sleep    3. Right now the dog is _____.

give    4. The boy is _____ out paper.

walk    5. Everyone is _____ as fast as possible.

try    6. I am _____ to learn to ride a bike.

grade    7. The teacher was _____ some papers.

jump    8. They were _____ on the bed.

practice    9. Ira was _____ making baskets.

build    10. The members are _____ a new church.

# 26

# The Verb BE

Am, is, are, was and were are forms of the verb be. Write the correct form of the be verb in the blank spaces. The first one is done for you.

**The Rule**

1. The horses ___are/were___ in their stable.

2. Tom _____ angry sometimes.

3. I _____ a leader in gym.

4. We _____ at the new ice cream store.

5. The black pony _____ by the creek.

6. Mina _____ small and dainty.

7. My brother _____ at Len's birthday party yesterday.

8. The cowboys _____ skillful riders.

9. I _____ sick last week.

10. That pavement _____ hot.

11. Maria and Ken _____ sad that day.

**27**

# The ING Verb Form

**The Rule** Verbs ending in <u>ing</u> must have a form of the verb <u>be</u> (am, is, are, was or were) in front of them.

Write the correct form of <u>be</u> in the sentences below.

1. Marta _____ running a fever today.

2. In the parks the flowers _____ budding.

3. The fire chief _____ working hard yesterday.

4. The family _____ getting ready for the picnic.

5. We _____ going shopping when the accident happened.

6. I _____ having a party today.

7. I _____ going to have the party earlier, but I couldn't.

8. A while ago the girls _____ rushing down the street on roller skates.

## 28

# Unscrambling Sentences

The jumbled sentences below have no helping verbs. Add a helping verb and then write each sentence. The first one is done for you.

1. over   running   pony   That   meadow   the

   That pony is running over the meadow.

2. girls   sewing   finished   their   The

   _____

3. soon   will   concert   going   We   the   to

   _____

4. working   project   on   They   both   the

   _____

5. year   coming   school   The   to   end   an

   _____

6. hope   to   house   next   We   you
   come   our   Thursday

   _____

## 29

# First and Third Person Verbs

Change each sentence from first person (I) to third person (he, she). Also change the verb by adding <u>s</u> or <u>es</u>. The first one is done for you.

1. I play the guitar.

   He/She plays the guitar.

2. I often write to my cousin.

   _____

3. I plant seeds in a planter.

   _____

4. I like to eat chocolate cake.

   _____

5. I lose pennies all the time.

   _____

6. I catch the ball he throws.

   _____

7. I like cookies at any time.

   _____

8. I paint pictures for fun.

   _____

## 30

# Making Questions

Change these sentences into questions by moving the verb or the helping verb to the beginning of the sentence. The first one is done for you.

1. We could try to wash the windows.

   Could we try to wash the windows?

2. The blue toy might be too expensive.

   _____

3. The new exhibit was one of the best.

   _____

4. Coal is one of our resources.

   _____

5. Both of the twins can swim well.

   _____

6. She doesn't understand the work.

   _____

7. The children will see the puppets.

   _____

**31**

# Noun or Verb?

As you read each pair of sentences, decide whether the underlined word has been used as a noun or as a verb. Then write <u>noun</u> or <u>verb</u> on the blank at the end of each sentence.

| | |
|---|---|
| Ex. Please put these crayons into the <u>box</u>. | noun |
| He thinks he wants to <u>box</u> professionally. | verb |

1. What kind of <u>duck</u> is that brown one? _____

   I do not know why, but I <u>duck</u> every time I hear thunder. _____

2. He works at a task as long as it takes to <u>master</u> it. _____

   The dog was happy to find his <u>master</u>. _____

3. I really do not like to have to pay the <u>rent</u>. _____

   Why don't you <u>rent</u> the equipment at the Sports Palace? _____

4. We plan to <u>feature</u> some real talent in our show. _____

   What is on the double <u>feature</u> tonight? _____

**32**

# Same Word - Different Use

Choose a word from the box that fits in both sentences of each pair. Write it on the blank line. Then write <u>N</u> where the word is used as a noun and <u>V</u> where it is used as a verb. The first one is done for you.

| ship | paint | light |
|------|-------|-------|
| dream | water | hammer |

1. __N__   We have some red ___paint___.
   __V__   They can ___paint___ our house.

2. _____   Get a _____ so we can see.
   _____   That bulb will _____ the room.

3. _____   The company will _____ the books.
   _____   There was a _____ on the ocean.

4. _____   The carpenter will _____ in the nails.
   _____   Be careful with that _____!

5. _____   I really need a drink of _____.
   _____   Let's _____ the lawn.

6. _____   It is nice to have a happy _____.
   _____   Do you _____ much?

*On to step 2*

You have finished

Step 1

## 33

# Adjectives

**The Rule**  **adjective: a word which modifies (names one of the characteristics of) a noun.**

### red bird - big dog - old lady

One noun in each of the following sentences has been circled. Underline each adjective that modifies the circled noun.

Ex. <u>A</u> <u>cold</u>, <u>wet</u> (snow) fell all day long.

1. We saw a big brown (bear.)

2. Ten good (players) struck out.

3. It was a cold and stormy (night.)

4. This is the best chocolate (cake.)

5. It weighs several (tons.)

6. Close the big screen (door.)

7. Where is the old red (hen?)

8. A tall dark (man) left a message.

9. An elderly, gray-haired (lady) got on the bus.

10. Where is the big, old, gray (dog) that used to wait at the gate?

## 34

# Adjectives

**Adjectives modify nouns by telling:**
   **a) which one (this, that, those, any, each)** **The Rule**
   **b) how many (several, one, all)**
   **c) what kind (big, yellow, old, pretty)**

Underline each adjective in the following sentences. Write <u>a</u>, <u>b</u>, or <u>c</u> on top of each adjective to show whether it tells a) which one, b) how many, or c) what kind.

>      a     b     c              a
> Ex. <u>Those</u> <u>four</u> <u>green</u> balls are on <u>the</u> table.

1. Several blue wagons are for sale.

2. He loves all little animals.

3. That large city is to the west.

4. All ten blue lamps were in boxes.

5. Any pretty red handkerchief will do.

6. She collects any old green pottery.

7. She has ten chipped red bricks.

8. They have two large new cars.

9. The little old lady walked across the street.

10. The helpful boy scout was not there.

**35**

# Adjectives

Choose an adjective from the box and write it on the blank line to complete each sentence.

| happy | narrow | thin |
|---|---|---|
| cold | | tall |

1. The _____ glass broke.

2. Keith is a _____ boy for his age.

3. My _____ friend laughed and joked.

4. That _____ trail leads up the mountain.

5. The _____ wind chilled all of us.

Circle the two adjectives in each sentence below.

6. The brown deer ate the green grass.

7. An exciting movie is fun.

8. This old pail is very rusty.

9. Those large animals are dangerous.

10. Our new neighbors are nice.

## 36

# Adjectives

Use the adjectives given to complete the sentences below. Add <u>er</u> or <u>est</u> to the adjectives if necessary. The first one is done for you.

| | |
|---|---|
| tall | 1. Carlos is the ____tallest____ boy in the room. |

new | 2. His bike is _____ than mine.

blue | 3. That is the _____ water I've seen.

dirty | 4. My shoes seem to be_____.

hot | 5. The sun seems _____ today than yesterday.

green | 6. There were three _____ boats on the lake.

funny | 7. I think that clown is _____ than the other one.

soft | 8. The blanket is the _____ one I've found.

ripe | 9. Is that apple _____ than this one?

fluffy | 10. The_____snow is falling down.

fuzzy | 11. This material is _____ than that over there.

delicious | 12. Rob thinks the cookies are _____.

**37**

# More Adjectives

The adjectives in the following sentences are underlined. Draw an arrow from each adjective to the noun or pronoun that it modifies. Then write what the adjective tells about the noun or pronoun: What kind, Which one, How much, or How many.

1. I paid the clerk <u>ten</u> dollars. _____

2. Carl is in <u>fifth</u> grade. _____

3. Everyone loves a <u>sunny</u> day. _____

4. The sweater is <u>new</u>. _____

5. The game lasted <u>several</u> hours. _____

6. <u>These</u> rocks were found on the moon.

   _____

7. Only a <u>few</u> people were invited. _____

8. She is a <u>fast</u> runner. _____

9. You certainly were <u>lucky</u>. _____

## 38

# Predicate Adjectives

The Rule

<u>predicate adjective</u>: an adjective that follows the verb in a sentence:

**Mark is <u>tall</u>.     Jane's hand is <u>cold</u>.**

Draw an arrow from the predicate adjective to the noun it describes.

Ex. The food tastes (good).

1. That suspect must be guilty.

2. The music sounds strange.

3. The baby appears tired.

4. This little town remains friendly.

5. Diane became discouraged.

6. The sky is growing black.

7. Grandfather's hair stays brown.

8. The casserole tastes delicious.

9. The crowd sounds happy.

10. The juniper will remain green.

11. This fabric feels scratchy.

12. Roses smell good.

## 39

# Adjectives and Predicate Adjectives

**The Rule** adjective: a word that modifies (names one of the characteristics of) a noun.

Adjectives precede the noun they modify:
<u>big</u>, <u>yellow</u> taxi

predicate adjective: an adjective that follows the verb in a sentence.

The taxi is <u>big</u> and <u>yellow</u>.

Underline the adjectives in the following sentences. Circle the predicate adjectives. Draw an arrow from each predicate adjective to the nouns they modify.

Ex. <u>All</u> hobbies are (fun)

1. Some flowers are blue.

2. Some games are educational.

3. Green trees are alive.

4. Red grapes are my favorite.

5. These kits are easy.

6. Cincinnati's catcher is tired.

7. The older daughter is a painter.

8. Those puppies are tiny.

# 40

# Adverbs

Adverbs answer the questions <u>how</u>, <u>when</u> and <u>where</u>. Underline each adverb in the sentences below. The first one is done for you.

1. They walked <u>quickly</u>.

2. Mother will go tomorrow.

3. It is cold outside.

4. Jan could sing well.

5. We should go now.

6. All of us went inside.

7. Later Joe will play.

8. Mother went to the store first.

9. You will find us there.

10. Slowly we worked on the picture.

11. The newspaper arrived late.

12. The wind was blowing hard.

13. Recently we heard about a new park.

14. This is certainly not finished.

**41**

# Adverbs

Underline each adverb. Draw an arrow to the verb it modifies. The first one is done for you.

1. Chico rides his bike <u>fast</u>.

2. My aunt left yesterday.

3. We think we'll go soon.

4. He has left with the guests already.

5. Tomorrow we'll have to leave.

6. Jane never finishes her jobs.

7. We tried walking backwards on the white line.

8. Soon they'll get a new car.

9. Then the program was done.

10. The swing suddenly rocked.

The Homework Booklet

# TUTOR'S GUIDE
# Grammar Level 4

This answer section has been placed in the center of this Homework Booklet so it can be easily removed if you so desire.

The solutions in this manual reflect the layout of the exercises to simplify checking.

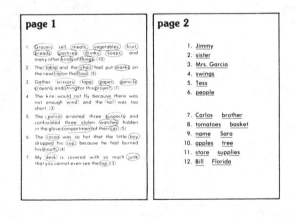

A motivational award is provided on the inside back cover. It has been designed to be signed by the tutor, either a parent or teacher.

**Motivational suggestion:** After the student completes each step, mark the achievement by placing a sticker next to that step shown on the award.

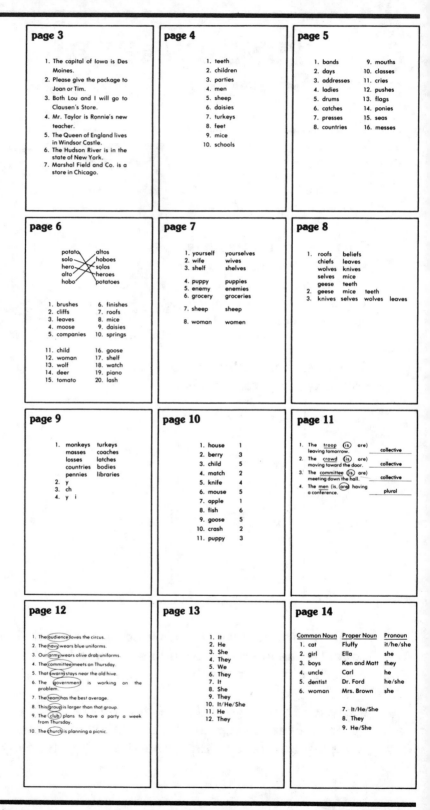

## Solutions

### page 3

1. The capital of Iowa is Des Moines.
2. Please give the package to Joan or Tim.
3. Both Lou and I will go to Clausen's Store.
4. Mr. Taylor is Ronnie's new teacher.
5. The Queen of England lives in Windsor Castle.
6. The Hudson River is in the state of New York.
7. Marshal Field and Co. is a store in Chicago.

### page 4

1. teeth
2. children
3. parties
4. men
5. sheep
6. daisies
7. turkeys
8. feet
9. mice
10. schools

### page 5

1. bands
2. days
3. addresses
4. ladies
5. drums
6. catches
7. presses
8. countries
9. mouths
10. classes
11. cries
12. pushes
13. flags
14. ponies
15. seas
16. messes

### page 6

potato — potatoes
solo — solos
hero — heroes
alto — altos
hobo — hoboes

1. brushes
2. cliffs
3. leaves
4. moose
5. companies
6. finishes
7. roofs
8. mice
9. daisies
10. springs

11. child
12. woman
13. wolf
14. deer
15. tomato
16. goose
17. shelf
18. watch
19. piano
20. lash

### page 7

1. yourself — yourselves
2. wife — wives
3. shelf — shelves
4. puppy — puppies
5. enemy — enemies
6. grocery — groceries
7. sheep — sheep
8. woman — women

### page 8

1. roofs — beliefs
   chiefs — leaves
   wolves — knives
   selves — mice
   geese — teeth
2. geese   mice   teeth
3. knives   selves   wolves   leaves

### page 9

1. monkeys   turkeys
   masses   coaches
   losses   latches
   countries   bodies
   pennies   libraries
2. y
3. ch
4. y i

### page 10

1. house — 1
2. berry — 3
3. child — 5
4. match — 2
5. knife — 4
6. mouse — 5
7. apple — 1
8. fish — 6
9. goose — 5
10. crash — 2
11. puppy — 3

### page 11

1. The troop (is) are) leaving tomorrow.   collective
2. The crowd (is) are) moving toward the door.   collective
3. The committee (is) are) meeting down the hall.   collective
4. The men (is, (are) having a conference.   plural

### page 12

1. The audience loves the circus.
2. The navy wears blue uniforms.
3. Our army wears olive drab uniforms.
4. The committee meets on Thursday.
5. That swarm stays near the old hive.
6. The government is working on the problem.
7. The team has the best average.
8. This group is larger than that group.
9. The club plans to have a party a week from Thursday.
10. The church is planning a picnic.

### page 13

1. It
2. He
3. She
4. They
5. We
6. They
7. It
8. She
9. They
10. It/He/She
11. He
12. They

### page 14

| Common Noun | Proper Noun | Pronoun |
| --- | --- | --- |
| 1. cat | Fluffy | it/he/she |
| 2. girl | Ella | she |
| 3. boys | Ken and Matt | they |
| 4. uncle | Carl | he |
| 5. dentist | Dr. Ford | he/she |
| 6. woman | Mrs. Brown | she |
| 7. | | It/He/She |
| 8. | | They |
| 9. | | He/She |

©1983, Instructional Fair, Inc.

## page 15

1. him
2. them
3. him
4. us
5. it
6. me
7. it
8. you
9. us
10. them
11. it
12. you

## page 16

1. us
2. them
3. her
4. him
5. me
6. it
7. us
8. him  her
9. them
10. me

## page 17

1. them
2. it
3. her
4. it
5. us
6. him
7. it
8. us/them
9. them

## page 18

Which pronouns were used as an adjective before a noun? my, your, its, his, their

Which pronouns can be used instead of a noun? mine, yours, its, his, theirs

Which pronouns can be used both with a noun and alone? its, his

## page 19

1. Where are ~~me~~ my shoes?
2. The dog is ~~ours~~ ours.
3. Is that ~~they're~~ their cat?
4. Do not play with ~~he~~ his toys.
5. ~~Me~~ My foot hurts.
6. ~~Ours~~ Our house is green.
7. Which one is ~~yours~~ yours?

## page 20

1. Birds (build) nests in the spring.
2. This product (scrubs) best.
3. We (plant) gardens in the spring.
4. It (rains) every evening here.
5. We (bought) a new car.
6. Our baseball team (practices) twice a week during baseball season.
7. They (fished) all day.
8. He (shoveled) all the snow away.
9. They (ice-skate) very well.
10. We (rode) our bicycles into town.
11. Jerry (bought) a new shirt.
12. We (raked) all of the leaves.
13. The dog (barked) all night.
14. Jan (baked) a cake.
15. The Clarks (painted) their house.

## page 21

1. He swims in the pool.
2. She bakes cookies on Monday.
3. It crawls in the grass.
4. He likes chocolate cake.
5. She plants flowers in the spring.
6. He enjoys helping at the zoo.

## page 22

1. sorted
2. cried
3. closed
4. burned
5. dared
6. fried
7. pushed
8. crossed
9. worried
10. carried
11. sipped
12. begged
13. liked
14. baked
15. spied
16. stopped

## page 23

1. (~~will~~, has) turned
2. (~~had~~, ~~have~~) moved
3. (~~has~~, have) become
4. (were, ~~was~~) skating
5. (have, ~~has~~) gone
6. (were, ~~has~~) eating
7. (~~have~~, has) planted
8. (have, ~~were~~) eaten
9. (has, ~~was~~) remained
10. (was, ~~will~~) listening

## page 24

1. visited
2. hunted
3. climbed
4. closed
5. picked
6. cheered
7. tasted
8. planted
9. washed
10. pulled

## page 25

1. We plant a garden; we _____ a garden tomorrow.     shall plant
2. We bake bread; we _____ bread tomorrow.     shall bake
3. We can vegetables; we _____ tomorrow.     shall can
4. He waters the plants; he _____ the plants tomorrow.     will water

## page 26

1. were dancing
2. was singing
3. is sleeping
4. is giving
5. is walking
6. am trying
7. was grading
8. were jumping
9. was practicing
10. are building

**Solutions**

# Solutions

## page 27

1. are/were
2. is/was
3. am/was
4. were/are
5. is/was
6. is/was
7. was
8. are/were
9. was
10. is/was
11. were

## page 28

1. is
2. are/were
3. was
4. is/was
5. were
6. am
7. was
8. were

## page 29

1. That pony is running over the meadow.
2. The girls have finished their sewing.
3. We will soon be going to the concert.
4. They are / were both working on the project.
5. The school year was/is coming to an end.
6. We hope you will come to our house next Thursday.

## page 30

1. He/She plays the guitar.
2. She/He often writes to her/his cousin.
3. He/She plants seeds in a planter.
4. She/He likes to eat chocolate cake.
5. He/She loses pennies all the time.
6. She/He catches the ball he throws.
7. He/She likes cookies at any time.
8. She/He paints pictures for fun.

## page 31

1. Could we try to wash the windows?
2. Might the blue toy be too expensive?
3. Was the new exhibit one of the best?
4. Is coal one of our resources?
5. Can both of the twins swim well?
6. Doesn't she understand the work?
7. Will the children see the puppets?

## page 32

1. What kind of _duck_ is that brown one? — noun
   I do not know why, but I _duck_ every time I hear thunder. — verb
2. He _works_ at a task as long as it takes to master it. — verb
   The dog was happy to find his _master_. — noun
3. I really do not like to have to pay the _rent_. — noun
   Why don't you _rent_ the equipment at the Sports Palace? — verb
4. We plan to _feature_ some real talent in our show. — verb
   What is on the double _feature_ tonight? — noun

## page 33

1. _N_ We have some red <u>paint</u>.
   _V_ They can <u>paint</u> our house.
2. _N_ Get a <u>light</u> so we can see.
   _V_ That bulb will <u>light</u> the room.
3. _V_ The company will <u>ship</u> the books.
   _N_ There was a <u>ship</u> on the ocean.
4. _V_ The carpenter will <u>hammer</u> in the nails.
   _N_ Be careful with that <u>hammer</u>!
5. _N_ I really need a drink of <u>water</u>.
   _V_ Let's <u>water</u> the lawn.
6. _N_ It is nice to have a happy <u>dream</u>.
   _V_ Do you <u>dream</u> much?

## page 34

1. We saw <u>a big brown bear</u>.
2. Ten good <u>players</u> struck out.
3. It was <u>a cold and stormy night</u>.
4. This is <u>the best chocolate cake</u>.
5. It weighs <u>several tons</u>.
6. Close <u>the big screen door</u>.
7. Where is <u>the old red hen</u>?
8. <u>A tall dark man</u> left a message.
9. <u>An elderly, gray-haired lady</u> got on the bus.
10. Where is <u>the big, old, gray dog</u> that used to wait at the gate?

## page 35

1. Several $\overset{b}{\text{blue}}$ $\overset{c}{\text{wagons}}$ are for sale.
2. He loves $\overset{b}{\text{all}}$ $\overset{c}{\text{little}}$ animals.
3. That $\overset{a}{\text{large}}$ $\overset{b}{\text{city}}$ is to the $\overset{a}{\text{west}}$.
4. All ten $\overset{b}{\text{blue}}$ $\overset{c}{\text{lamps}}$ were in boxes.
5. Any pretty $\overset{a}{\text{red}}$ $\overset{c}{\text{handkerchief}}$ will do.
6. She collects $\overset{a}{\text{any}}$ $\overset{c}{\text{old}}$ $\overset{c}{\text{green}}$ pottery.
7. She has $\overset{b}{\text{ten}}$ $\overset{c}{\text{chipped}}$ $\overset{c}{\text{red}}$ bricks.
8. They have $\overset{a}{\text{two}}$ $\overset{c}{\text{large}}$ $\overset{c}{\text{new}}$ cars.
9. The $\overset{a}{\text{little}}$ $\overset{c}{\text{old}}$ lady walked across the $\overset{a}{\text{street}}$.
10. The $\overset{a}{\text{helpful}}$ $\overset{c}{\text{boy}}$ scout was not there.

## page 36

1. thin
2. tall
3. happy
4. narrow
5. cold

6. brown   green
7. exciting   fun
8. old   rusty
9. large   dangerous
10. new   nice

## page 37

1. tallest
2. newer
3. bluest
4. dirty
5. hotter
6. green
7. funnier
8. softest
9. riper
10. fluffy
11. fuzzier
12. delicious

## page 38

1. ten dollars — How many
2. fifth grade — Which one
3. sunny day — What kind
4. sweater new — What kind
5. several hours — How many
6. These rocks — Which ones
7. few people — How many
8. fast runner — What kind
9. You lucky — What kind

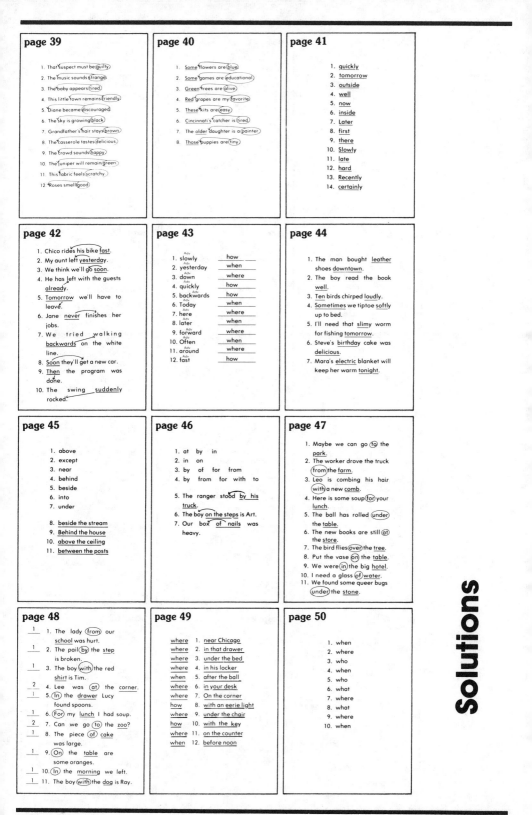

## page 39

1. That suspect must be (guilty).
2. The music sounds (strange).
3. The baby appears (tired).
4. This little town remains (friendly).
5. Diane became (discouraged).
6. The sky is growing (black).
7. Grandfather's hair stays (brown).
8. The casserole tastes (delicious).
9. The crowd sounds (happy).
10. The juniper will remain (green).
11. This fabric feels (scratchy).
12. Roses smell (good).

## page 40

1. Some (flowers) are (blue).
2. Some (games) are (educational).
3. Green (trees) are (alive).
4. Red (grapes) are my (favorite).
5. These (kits) are (easy).
6. Cincinnati's (catcher) is (tired).
7. The older (daughter) is a (painter).
8. Those (puppies) are (tiny).

## page 41

1. quickly
2. tomorrow
3. outside
4. well
5. now
6. inside
7. Later
8. first
9. there
10. Slowly
11. late
12. hard
13. Recently
14. certainly

## page 42

1. Chico rides his bike fast.
2. My aunt left yesterday.
3. We think we'll go soon.
4. He has left with the guests already.
5. Tomorrow we'll have to leave.
6. Jane never finishes her jobs.
7. We tried walking backwards on the white line.
8. Soon they'll get a new car.
9. Then the program was done.
10. The swing suddenly rocked.

## page 43

| | Adv | |
|---|---|---|
| 1. | slowly | how |
| 2. | yesterday | when |
| 3. | down | where |
| 4. | quickly | how |
| 5. | backwards | how |
| 6. | Today | when |
| 7. | here | where |
| 8. | later | when |
| 9. | forward | where |
| 10. | Often | when |
| 11. | around | where |
| 12. | fast | how |

## page 44

1. The man bought leather shoes downtown.
2. The boy read the book well.
3. Ten birds chirped loudly.
4. Sometimes we tiptoe softly up to bed.
5. I'll need that slimy worm for fishing tonight.
6. Steve's birthday cake was delicious.
7. Mara's electric blanket will keep her warm tonight.

## page 45

1. above
2. except
3. near
4. behind
5. beside
6. into
7. under

8. beside the stream
9. Behind the house
10. above the ceiling
11. between the posts

## page 46

1. at    by    in
2. in    on
3. by    of    for    from
4. by    from    for    with    to
5. The ranger stood by his truck.
6. The boy on the steps is Art.
7. Our box of nails was heavy.

## page 47

1. Maybe we can go (to) the park.
2. The worker drove the truck (from) the farm.
3. Leo is combing his hair (with) a new comb.
4. Here is some soup (for) your lunch.
5. The ball has rolled (under) the table.
6. The new books are still (at) the store.
7. The bird flies (over) the tree.
8. Put the vase (on) the table.
9. We were (in) the big hotel.
10. I need a glass (of) water.
11. We found some queer bugs (under) the stone.

## page 48

1   1. The lady (from) our school was hurt.
1   2. The pail (by) the step is broken.
1   3. The boy (with) the red shirt is Tim.
2   4. Lee was (at) the corner.
1   5. (In) the drawer Lucy found spoons.
1   6. (For) my lunch I had soup.
2   7. Can we go (to) the zoo?
1   8. The piece (of) cake was large.
1   9. (On) the table are some oranges.
1   10. (In) the morning we left.
1   11. The boy (with) the dog is Ray.

## page 49

where   1. near Chicago
where   2. in that drawer
where   3. under the bed
where   4. in his locker
when    5. after the ball
where   6. in your desk
where   7. On the corner
how     8. with an eerie light
where   9. under the chair
how     10. with the key
where   11. on the counter
when    12. before noon

## page 50

1. when
2. where
3. who
4. when
5. who
6. what
7. where
8. what
9. where
10. when

## Solutions

## page 51

**A Man on the Moon**

Adv       N      V
Slowly the rocket lifted into

                       V      V
space. It was going to the

 N                   Adv
moon. The rocket went quickly

        N
on its way. "The moon looks
              Adj
like a bright ball," said an

astronaut. The astronauts
 V                  Adj
landed. Everything was quiet.

## page 52

1. the patiently green sat parrot
   The green parrot sat patiently.
2. grass the profusely green grew
   The green grass grew profusely.
3. large the thunderously oak fell
   The large oak fell thunderously.
4. the screamed angry man loudly
   The angry man screamed loudly.
5. widely the yawned bored class
   The bored class yawned widely.
6. sang canary loudly the energetic
   The energetic canary sang loudly.

## page 53

| Nouns | | Pronouns |
|---|---|---|
| fielder | air | it |
| batter | plate | he |
| ball | pitcher | she |
| bat | swing | |

| Adjectives | Adverbs |
|---|---|
| white | then |
| small | hard |
| new | high |

| Verbs | | Prepositions |
|---|---|---|
| grabbed | hit | with |
| watched | went | at |
| threw | | in |
| | | of |

## page 54

1. Jerry and Benny
2. apple or a banana
3. London and Paris
4. brother and I
5. pen or a pencil
6. Carl or Mike
7. Mother and Dad
8. sister and brother
9. lake and the river
10. boys and girls

## page 55

1. The goat followed me back.
2. This yellow pencil just broke.
3. Sam jumped aside quickly.
   or
   Sam quickly jumped aside.
4. Matt likes chocolate chip cookies.
5. My old watch still runs.
6. Soon it will be New Year's Eve.
7. The tallest buildings are downtown.
8. Our best player is Tommy.

## page 56

1. My sister Mary works in a store.
2. The bike in the garage belongs to me.
3. The contest at school ends tomorrow.
4. Six of the boys in my class went on a trip.
5. John rides his bike to school.
6. All of us like sports and games.
7. We went on a field trip to the museum.
8. Sue and Mary made a present for their mother.

## page 57

1. Her sister | wrote a letter to her.
2. Louis | caught the biggest fish.
3. The rider | went into the mountains.
4. The bear | stood on its hind legs.
5. My friend | sails the family boat every weekend.
6. The scissors | need sharpening.
7. The boys | left the bicycle out in the rain.
8. Rosie | studies her lessons at night.
9. Tom | plans to attend the game.
10. Several children | sing in the choir.
11. Elton | plays with his puppies.

## page 58

1. That lion | roared at me.
2. The children | picked pretty flowers.
3. Our family | took a bus trip to the zoo.
4. The neighbors | built a fence for the dog.
5. Kate's bike | needs new tires.
6. Dan's dad | gave him a new softball.
7. Those people | stayed at the motel.
8. Their new jeep | goes up steep hills.
9. Skateboards | are sometimes dangerous.
10. That shop | has twenty-seven flavors of ice cream.

## page 59

1. The little birds | sang sweet songs.
2. The striped ball | rolled away.
3. The family | ate all the fruit.
4. Mother | rocked in her chair.
5. The boats | carried people on the river.
6. The circus | had a big parade.
7. The class | went on a picnic.
8. Two little dogs | played together.
9. Those monkeys | did many cute tricks.
10. The bell | rang a long time ago.
11. Marie | saw six sailboats on the lake.
12. The grocer | sells many different kinds of things.

## page 60

Cherries can be kept for making tarts at Christmas without preserving. Take the fairest cherries you can find, fresh from the trees. Be careful not to bruise them. Wipe them one by one with a linen cloth. Then put them into a barrel of hay. Place them in layers, first laying hay on the bottom, and then cherries and then hay and then cherries and then hay again. Fill the barrel as close to the top as possible so that no air can get to them. Then set them under a feather bed where someone always sleeps every night, because the warmer they are kept, the better it is. But they should not be kept near the fire. If you do this, you may have fresh cherries any time of the year.

## page 61

"What would you call an orange polka dot horse?" asked Fred.

"Well," Alfred decided, "I'd call that a horse of a different color."

Fred asked, "Do you think a man could starve in the Arabian Desert?"

Alfred reasoned, "How could he with all the sandwiches (sand which is) there?"

"What did the adding machine say?" asked Fred.

"You can count on me," answered Alfred.

Tell me why a healthy person is like the United States," said Fred.

"Is it because they both have a good constitution?" guessed Alfred.

Fred asked, "What would you call a choirboy who rips his outfit?"

"Well," decided Alfred, "I'd call him a holy tearer."

## page 62

1. The only place I have been able to find Watkin's Licorice is Brown's Drugstore on Maple Street.
2. The Raymonds are trying to teach their dogs, Barkley and Arfer, to guard the house.
3. He has cards at both the Chesterfield Library and at the Frankfort Library.
4. Frankie is moving to Wisconsin.
5. Do we plan to have lunch at Green Tree Restaurant or at Christmas's?
6. She works for the Red Cross.
7. Let's go to Little Putt Golfland.
8. We are trying to get Greener's Meat Market to sponsor our team.

### page 63

1. No, I do not think Aunt Mary likes this kind of cake.
2. Wait and I will see if Doctor is busy.
3. Jack named his goat, Nose.
4. Just a minute, I'll ask Mother if she needs help with the party.
5. When did Uncle Sam become the symbol for this country?
6. My cousin, Fred, and his dog, Trigger, are practicing circus tricks.
7. If Mr. Wills doesn't come for that vase soon, you may give it to your mother.
8. Let's ask Father to fix this bicycle.

### page 64

1. Our teacher graduated from Princeton University.
2. Who is our district's representative in the House of Representatives?
3. Linda's mother has decided to call her new store, Plants for Aunts and Others.
4. Will the Boy Scouts of America have a booth at the fair this summer?
5. He belongs to the Elks' Club, not to the Lions' Club.
6. Meet me at the Plaza Theater.

### page 65

1. He used to be a Republican but switched to the Democratic Party about two years ago.
2. We spoke in French and we could find no one who spoke English.
3. The Methodist, Baptist, and Catholic churches are all located at the same corner.
4. Everyone says that pizza did not originate in Italy, but almost every Italian restaurant I have ever seen serves pizza.
5. After taking Black Studies, I can understand Swahili but I cannot speak it.
6. She is looking for a good Chinese cookbook.

### page 66

1. Sometimes I wish I could have lived during the Middle Ages.
2. Plaster casts for broken limbs were developed during the Crimean War.
3. We will be reading about the Magna Carta tomorrow.
4. The first ten amendments to the Constitution are usually referred to as the Bill of Rights.
5. This record of Medieval music is very interesting.
6. Some of the most beautiful works of art were created during the Renaissance.
7. The Civil War is known officially as the War of the Rebellion.

### page 67

1. They are planning a trip to London, England next fall.
2. It seems that there is always some kind of trouble in at least one of the Asian countries.
3. We saw Hoover Dam on our trip to the Rocky Mountains last summer.
4. My sister was surprised that the Gulf of Mexico looked just like the Atlantic Ocean off the coast of Florida.
5. Last year we went to Yellowstone Park, and this year we plan to go to Lake Michigan.
6. They live in Madison County, about a mile west of Tylerville.

### page 68

1. Jack could not read enough about the Old West.
2. Do you think our next president is more likely to come from the Northeast or from the Southwest?
3. Now, this is hospitality like I remember from the Deep South.
4. Which states are in the Midwest?
5. What do you know about the most recent crisis in the Middle East?
6. The Civil War was more complicated than just that the North and the South did not get along.

### page 69

1. Mindy likes to sit in front of the mirror and practice smiling like the Mona Lisa.
2. Which did you enjoy more, the book titled Tom Sawyer or the movie version?
3. Janet's father likes to buy a copy of the Sunday edition of the New York Times.
4. Do we really have to memorize the Declaration of Independence?
5. Randy wants a subscription to the National Geographic for his birthday.

### page 70

1. My brother always gets his Halloween costume ready the Saturday before he needs it.
2. December, January, and February are warm months in Chile.
3. Are Passover and Easter the same week this year?
4. The mailman does not deliver mail on Sunday.
5. He works Saturday and Sunday but gets Monday and Tuesday off.
6. Do you plan to have turkey for Thanksgiving?
7. Do you have any special activities planned for Book Week?

### page 71

1. We drove through the Blue Ridge Mountains on our way to Washington D.C.
2. Janet has a dog named Rover Woolsey.
3. How far is it from New Orleans, Louisiana to Little Rock, Arkansas?
4. The closest place to buy Wilson's Chocolates is at the Green Parrot Drugstore in Johnson City.
5. We do not know whether to vote for Ralph Arthur or for Sam Rubenstein.
6. We crossed the Missouri River in Montana.
7. The first time he left New York, he went all the way to Paris, France.
8. Meet us at the American Theater.
9. He joined the Boy Scouts.
10. They are Canadians.

### page 72

The Flag Goes By
by Henry Holcomb Bennett

Hats off!
Along the street there comes
A blare of bugles, a ruffle of drums,
A flash of color beneath the sky:
Hats off!
The flag is passing by!

Blue and crimson and white it shines,
Over the steel-tipped, ordered lines,
Hats off!
The colors before us fly;
But more than the flag is passing by:

. . . . .

Sign of a nation, great and strong
To ward her people from foreign wrong:
Pride and glory and honor—all
Live in the colors to stand or fall.

. . . . .

### page 73

Many people like to prepare their own dried fruit. ⊙ c Sun drying is one of the easiest methods for drying fruit. ⊙ c - Just wash it, slice it, and lay it out in the sun. ⊙ c Of course, anything dries fastest on bright, hot breezy days. ⊙ c Use an electric fan to speed the drying process t ⓒ Test to be sure the fruit is dried. t ⓒ Fruit is dry enough if no moisture comes out when it is squeezed. ⊙ c

### page 74

Do you think that ostriches bury their heads in the sand? The fact is that they do not. Their heads are very small compared to their bodies. Is it possible that people who watched an ostrich eating simply could not see its head? They might have thought the ostriches' heads were buried in the sand. We do know that a frightened baby ostrich drops its body to the ground and gets its head as low as possible. Is that the instinct that made ancient people think that an ostrich buries its head in the sand?

## page 75

You must hear what happened to me when I was in the jungle! First I was walking along a quiet path. All of a sudden, I heard a noise that frightened me right out of my skin! It turned out to be only a small bird with a very big voice. Then I saw a huge shadow shaped like a bull elephant ready to charge! But that turned out to be a tree with one big branch sticking out from the rest. The most frightening thing of all was when I slipped over the edge of a cliff! That is when I woke up.

## page 76

1. Major Pierre Charles L'Enfant drew the original plans for Washington, District of Columbia.

2. The Mississippi begins near Lake Itaska, Minnesota.

3. The Country Music Hall of Fame is located in Nashville, Tennessee.

4. Buffalo Bill is buried on Lookout Mountain near Golden, Colorado.

5. The Mission of San Miguel which is probably the oldest church in the United States is located in Santa Fe, New Mexico.

## page 77

1. Alabama became a state on December 14, 1819.

2. It was November 8, 1889, that Montana became a state.

3. On June 1, 1792, Kentucky became a state.

4. Alaska did not become a state until January 3, 1959.

5. Idaho has been a state since July 3, 1890.

6. Wyoming joined the Union on July 10, 1890.

## page 78

1. Dear Anita , 　　May 13, 1925

　　Sincerely ,
　　Margaret

2. Dear Pedro , 　　March 18, 1951

　　Yours truly ,
　　Jason

3. Dear Mom , 　　July 4, 1976

　　Your son ,
　　Aaron

## page 79

48 Reverberation Ave.
Sophistication, CA 94199
April 15, 1979

Dear Aunt Rhonda,

José and I can hardly wait until your visit! When will your bus arrive ? We have to know so we can meet you .

We thought we would miss the farm when we moved . But we all really love this city ! (.) We like being so close to the ocean, too . (!) By the way, how is everything on the farm ?

The first thing we will do when you get unpacked is go to the beach ! (.) Have you ever seen the ocean ? Don't forget your swimming suit ! (.)

Please hurry !

　　Your niece,
　　Maria

## page 80

1. Sur  Mon.  Tues.  Wed. Thur.  Fri.  Sat.

2. Jan.  Feb.  Mar.  Apr. Aug.  Sept.  Oct.  Nov. Dec.

3. February  Tuesday September  Wednesday

## page 81

1. Dec.
2. Fri.
3. Mr.
4. St.
5. U. S.
6. Sun.
7. Dr.
8. Ave.
9. Co.
10. Aug.

## page 82

1. Be sure to watch Gov. Michaels this eve. at 6 p.m.

2. field trip this Thurs.

3. Aunt Betty's baby was born at 4:50 a.m and weighed 7 lbs. and 6 oz.

4. need to buy 1 doz eggs and 1 pt of cream for angel food cake and icing

5. Vacation starts first Mon. in Aug.

## page 83

1. John Fitzgerald Kennedy    J. F. K.
2. Parent Teacher Association    P.T.A.
3. registered nurse    R.N.
4. intelligence quotient    I.Q.
5. Federal Bureau of Investigation    F.B.I.
6. Central Intelligence Agency    C.I.A.
7. Boy Scouts of America    B.S.A.
8. Franklin Delano Roosevelt    F. D. R.
9. Theodore Roosevelt    T. R.

## page 84

1. black
2. closely
3. cream
4. deed
5. fasten
6. freedom
7. frost
8. produce
9. solve
10. spread
11. team
12. train

13. cart closely cream debt
14. soap solve spread tame

## page 85

cause — /brij/
freeze — /ung'kal/
bridge — /kōz/
uncle — /blū/
blue — /frēz/

castle — /strānj/
strange — /cas'al/
choice — /chois/
tower — /rông/
wrong — /tou'ar/

## page 86

1. 2
2. 2
3. 3
4. 3

# More Adverbs

Write <u>Adv</u> over the adverb in each sentence. Then write <u>when</u>, <u>where</u> or <u>how</u> on each line to tell what question the adverb answers.

1. You are working rather slowly. _____

2. We went to the zoo yesterday. _____

3. Put that ball down. _____

4. She quickly ate the cake. _____

5. He can walk backwards. _____

6. Today Eli is sick. _____

7. We can both sit here. _____

8. You can play games later. _____

9. I can hop forward. _____

10. Often we ride in the car. _____

11. I was looking around. _____

12. Our swing can go fast. _____

## 43

# Adjectives and Adverbs

Use the words in the boxes to complete the sentences.

| Adjectives | |
| --- | --- |
| delicious | slimy |
| ten | leather |
| birthday | electric |

| Adverbs | |
| --- | --- |
| downtown | well |
| softly | loudly |
| sometimes | tonight |
| tomorrow | |

1. The  man  bought _____ shoes _____.

2. The boy read the book _____.

3. _____ birds chirped _____.

4. _____ we tiptoe _____ up to bed.

5. I'll need that _____ worm for fishing _____.

6. Steve's _____ cake was _____.

7. Mara's _____ blanket will keep her warm _____.

**44**

# Using Prepositions

Use one of the prepositions in the box to complete each sentence.

| | | | |
|---|---|---|---|
| beside | above | into | near |
| | except | behind | under |

1. The clouds are _____ us.

2. No one _____ Jan finished his report.

3. We live _____ the corner.

4. Don't back the car, there is something _____ it.

5. Who was that _____ the river?

6. My sister fell _____ the pool.

7. Look _____ the bed for the shoe.

Underline the prepositional phrases below.

8. The children were standing beside the stream.

9. Behind the house was a big yard.

10. What is above the ceiling?

11. Kick the ball between the posts.

**45**

# Prepositions

On the lines under each sentence write all the prepositions from the box that make sense in the sentence.

| at | in | on | for | with |
|----|----|----|-----|------|
| by | of | to | from | |

1. Are you _____ the house?

   _____ _____ _____

2. The ring was lost _____ the ground.

   _____ _____

3. That is a picture _____ her.

   _____ _____ _____ _____

4. The package is _____ him.

   _____ _____ _____ _____

Underline the prepositional phrases. Draw an arrow from the prepositional phrase to the word it tells something about. The first one is done for you.

5. The ranger stood by his truck.

6. The boy on the steps is Art.

7. Our box of nails was heavy.

The Homework Booklet

# Reviewing Prepositions

Circle the prepositions in each of the sentences. Underline the noun after the preposition. The first one is done for you.

| at | on | with | of | from |
|----|----|------|----|------|
| over | under | for | to | in |

1. Maybe we can go (to) the <u>park</u>.

2. The worker drove the truck from the farm.

3. Leo is combing his hair with a new comb.

4. Here is some soup for your lunch.

5. The ball has rolled under the table.

6. The new books are still at the store.

7. The bird flies over the tree.

8. Put the vase on the table.

9. We were in the big hotel.

10. I need a glass of water.

11. We found some queer bugs under the stone.

**47**

# Finding Prepositions and Their Nouns

Circle the preposition in each sentence. Underline the noun after it. Write <u>1</u> if the preposition is before the verb and <u>2</u> if it is after the verb. The first one is done for you.

<u>1</u>   1. The lady (from) our <u>school</u> was hurt.

_____  2. The pail by the step is broken.

_____  3. The boy with the red shirt is Tim.

_____  4. Lee was at the corner.

_____  5. In the drawer Lucy found spoons.

_____  6. For my lunch I had soup.

_____  7. Can we go to the zoo?

_____  8. The piece of cake was large.

_____  9. On the table are some oranges.

_____  10. In the morning we left.

_____  11. The boy with the dog is Ray.

## 48

    

# Prepositional Phrases

A prepositional phrase may be used as an adverb. Underline the prepositional phrases. On the line, write <u>how</u>, <u>when</u> or <u>where</u> to tell what question the phrase answers. The first one is done for you.

**The Rule**

| | | |
|---|---|---|
| where | 1. | The group is <u>near Chicago.</u> |
| _____ | 2. | Our pencils are in that drawer. |
| _____ | 3. | Your cat is under the bed. |
| _____ | 4. | His notebook was in his locker. |
| _____ | 5. | Cinderella lost her slipper after the ball. |
| _____ | 6. | Your math book is in your desk. |
| _____ | 7. | On the corner is that cute girl. |
| _____ | 8. | The ghost appeared with an eerie light. |
| _____ | 9. | The marble rolled under the chair. |
| _____ | 10. | The secret passage opened with a turn of the key. |
| _____ | 11. | The groceries are on the counter. |
| _____ | 12. | We can't be there before noon. |

**49**

# Prepositional Phrases

Write the words <u>where</u>, <u>when</u>, <u>what</u> or <u>who</u> to describe the underlined phrase on the line.

1. The group will leave <u>at 9:00 o'clock</u> A.M.

   _____

2. The kitten was sitting <u>on the porch</u>.

   _____

3. All <u>of the music group</u> will practice today.

   _____

4. We have math <u>in the morning</u>.

   _____

5. Members <u>of the club</u> will put on a show.

   _____

6. The box <u>of matches</u> got wet.

   _____

7. We will meet <u>at the corner</u>.

   _____

8. A bunch <u>of daisies</u> was in the vase.

   _____

9. The stream may be found <u>over the next hill</u>.

   _____

10. The tryouts will be held <u>during the next week</u>.

   _____

*You're doing great!*

You have finished

Step 2

## 50

# Parts of Speech

Read the story. Then identify the underlined words with these letters:

N—for noun—a person, place or thing.

V—for verb—shows action.

Adj —for adjective—answers the question, "What is it like?"

Adv —for adverb—answers where, how or when.

A Man on the Moon

<u>Slow</u>ly the <u>rocket</u> <u>lifted</u> into space. It was

<u>going</u> to the <u>moon</u>. The rocket went <u>quickly</u> on

its <u>way</u>. "The moon looks like a <u>bright</u> ball," <u>said</u>

an astronaut. The astronauts <u>landed.</u> Everything

was <u>quiet</u>.

**51**

# Scrambled Sentences

Number each word in the following groups according to this system:

articles - 1, adjectives - 2, nouns - 3,
verbs - 4, adverbs - 5.

Then copy the words in numerical order.

>      5     4   1    3    2
> Ex. quickly ran the rabbit little.
> The little rabbit ran quickly.

1. the patiently green sat parrot

   _____

2. grass the profusely green grew

   _____

3. large the thunderously oak fell

   _____

4. the screamed angry man loudly

   _____

5. widely the yawned bored class

   _____

6. sang canary loudly the energetic

   _____

# 52

# Classifying Words

Read the story. Find two different words from the story to write under each heading. One word has already been entered under each heading.

> **An Exciting Game**
> The small batter watched the white ball. The new pitcher threw it at the plate. With a swing of the bat, he hit that ball hard. High in the air it went. The fielder watched. Then she grabbed the ball.

Nouns
fielder
_____
_____

Pronouns
it
_____
_____

Adjectives
white
_____
_____

Adverbs
then
_____
_____

Verbs
grabbed
_____
_____

Prepositions
with
_____
_____

**53**

# Compound Subjects

**The Rule**

When two or more subject nouns or pronouns are joined by <u>and</u> or <u>or</u>, the subject is <u>compound</u>. Underline the compound subject in the sentences below. The first one is done for you.

1. <u>Jerry</u> and <u>Benny</u> are going with their dad to camp.

2. An apple or a banana may be chosen for dessert.

3. London and Paris are large cities.

4. My brother and I both play the piano.

5. A pen or a pencil may be used for the work.

6. Probably Carl or Mike will win the prize.

7. Mother and Dad went golfing.

8. My sister and brother are helping me with reading.

9. The lake and the river are filled with water.

10. The boys and girls are at a carnival.

## 54

# Making Sentences

Use the words below to make sentences. The first one is done for you.

1. back followed goat The me

   The goat followed me back.

2. pencil yellow This broke just

   _____

3. quickly Sam aside jumped

   _____

4. cookies likes chocolate Matt chip

   _____

5. old still watch My runs

   _____

6. will be Soon New Year's Eve it

   _____

7. buildings are tallest The downtown

   _____

8. Tommy Our is player best

   _____

## 55

# Two Parts
# of a Sentence

**The Rule**   The <u>subject</u> of a sentence is the part about which something is said. Underline the subject in each sentence below.

1.   My sister Mary works in a store.

2.   The bike in the garage belongs to me.

3.   The contest at school ends tomorrow.

4.   Six of the boys in my class went on a trip.

**The Rule**   The <u>predicate</u> of a sentence is the part that tells about the subject. Underline the predicate in each sentence below.

5.   John rides his bike to school.

6.   All of us like sports and games.

7.   We went on a field trip to the museum.

8.   Sue and Mary made a present for their mother.

# 56

# Sentence Parts

In each sentence below write <u>N</u> over the subject noun and <u>V</u> over each verb. Draw a line between each subject and <u>predicate</u> (the part with the verb in it). The first one is done for you.

       N     V
1. Her sister | wrote a letter to her.

2. Louis caught the biggest fish.

3. The rider went into the mountains.

4. The bear stood on its hind legs.

5. My friend sails the family boat every weekend.

6. The scissors need sharpening.

7. The boys left the bicycle out in the rain.

8. Rosie studies her lessons at night.

9. Tom plans to attend the game.

10. Several children sing in the choir.

11. Elton plays with his puppies.

**57**

# Subject and Predicate

**The Rule** The subject of the sentence is usually near the beginning. The predicate of the sentence is the part that begins with the verb. Draw a line between the subject and predicate. Write <u>SN</u> over the subject noun. The first one is done for you.

> $\overset{\text{SN}}{}$
> 1. That lion | roared at me.

2. The children picked pretty flowers.

3. Our family took a bus trip to the zoo.

4. The neighbors built a fence for the dog.

5. Kate's bike needs new tires.

6. Dan's dad gave him a new softball.

7. Those people stayed at the motel.

8. Their new jeep goes up steep hills.

9. Skateboards are sometimes dangerous.

10. That shop has twenty-seven flavors of ice cream.

**58**

# Subject and Predicate

Draw a line between the subject and predicate. Write <u>SN</u> above the subject noun and <u>V</u> above the verb. The first one is done for you.

>         SN    V
> 1. The little birds | sang sweet songs.

2. The striped ball rolled away.

3. The family ate all the fruit.

4. Mother rocked in her chair.

5. The boats carried people on the river.

6. The circus had a big parade.

7. The class went on a picnic.

8. Two little dogs played together.

9. Those monkeys did many cute tricks.

10. The bell rang a long time ago.

11. Marie saw six sailboats on the lake.

12. The grocer sells many different kinds of things.

*Looking good!*

You have finished

Step 3

**59**

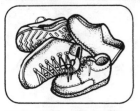

# First Word in a Sentence

**The Rule** The first word in every sentence is capitalized.

The following paragraph was adapted from the personal writings of Martha Washington. Capitalize the first word in every sentence.

Cherries can be kept for making tarts at Christmas without preserving.  take the fairest cherries you can find, fresh from the trees.  be careful not to bruise them.  wipe them one by one with a linen cloth.  then put them into a barrel of hay.  place them in layers, first laying hay on the bottom, and then cherries and then hay and then cherries and then hay again.  fill the barrel as close to the top as possible so that no air can get to them.  then set them under a feather bed where someone sleeps every night, because the warmer they are kept, the better it is.  but they should not be kept near the fire.  if you do this, you may have fresh cherries any time of the year.

**Begin Step 4** Language Skills

## 60

# Capitals and Quotations

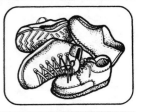

**The first word in a quoted sentence is capitalized.** **The Rule**

Capitalize the first word of each quoted sentence in the paragraphs below.

" What would you call an orange polka dot horse?" asked Fred.

" well," Alfred decided, "I'd call that a horse of a different color."

Fred asked, " do you think a man could starve in the Arabian Desert?"

Alfred reasoned, " how could he with all the sandwiches (sand which is) there?"

" what did the adding machine say?" asked Fred.

" you can count on me," answered Alfred.

" tell me why a healthy person is like the United States," said Fred.

" is it because they both have a good constitution?" guessed Alfred.

Fred asked, " what would you call a choirboy who rips his outfit?"

" well," decided Alfred, "I'd call him a holy tearer."

**61**

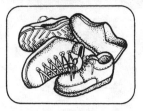

# Proper Nouns

**The Rule**

**proper noun:** a special name that refers to a specific person, group of persons, place, animal or thing.

**All proper nouns are capitalized.**

Capitalize the proper nouns in the following sentences.

1. The only place I have been able to find Watkin's licorice is Brown's drugstore on Maple Street.

2. The raymonds are trying to teach their dogs, barkley and arfer, to guard the house.

3. He has cards at both the chesterfield library and at the frankfort library.

4. frankie is moving to wisconsin.

5. Do we plan to have lunch at green tree restaurant or at christman's?

6. She works for the red cross.

7. Let's go to little putt golfland.

8. We are trying to get greener's meat market to sponsor our team.

**62**

©1983, Instructional Fair, Inc.

# Names, Titles, and "I"

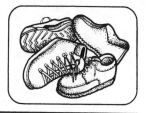

**Names of people and pets, and the nouns and titles such as Mother and Doctor which take the place of, or are used with names are capitalized. The pronoun, I, is also capitalized.**  **The Rule**

Capitalize the names of people and pets and the nouns that take the place of these names in the following sentences. Also, capitalize the pronoun, I.

1. No, I do not think Aunt Mary likes this kind of cake.

2. Wait and i will see if doctor is busy.

3. jack named his goat, hosé.

4. Just a minute, i'll ask mother if she needs help with the party.

5. When did uncle sam become the symbol for this country?

6. My cousin, fred, and his dog, trigger, are practicing circus tricks.

7. If mr. wills doesn't come for that vase soon, you may give it to your mother.

8. Let's ask father to fix this bicycle.

**63**

 ©1983, Instructional Fair, Inc.

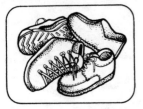

# Names of Groups

**The Rule** Names of organizations, business firms, institutions, and government bodies are capitalized. (Unimportant words such as "a", "an", "the", and, "of" etc. are usually not capitalized.)

Capitalize the names of organizations, businesses, institutions, and government bodies mentioned in the following sentences.

1. Our teacher graduated from Princeton University.

2. Who is our district's representative in the house of representatives?

3. Linda's mother has decided to call her new store, plants for aunts and others.

4. Will the boy scouts of america have a booth at the fair this summer?

5. He belongs to the elks' club, not to the lions' club.

6. Meet me at the plaza theater.

# Groups and Languages

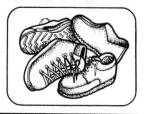

**Nationalities, languages, religions, and political parties and the adjectives derived from them are capitalized.**

Capitalize the name of each nationality, language, religion, or political party mentioned in the following sentences.

1. He used to be a Republican but switched to the Democratic Party about two years ago.

2. We spoke no french and we could find no one who spoke english.

3. The methodist, baptist, and catholic churches and the jewish synagogue are all located at the same corner.

4. Everyone says that pizza did not originate in Italy, but almost every italian restaurant I have ever seen serves pizza.

5. After taking black Studies, I can understand swahili but I cannot speak it.

6. She is looking for a good chinese cookbook.

**65**

©1983, Instructional Fair, Inc.

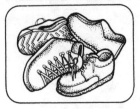

# Historical Terms

**The Rule** The names of historical events, historical documents, and periods in history are capitalized.

Capitalize the name of each historical event, document, or period mentioned in the following sentences.

1. Sometimes I wish I could have lived during the Middle Ages.

2. Plaster casts for broken limbs were developed during the crimean war.

3. We will be reading about the magna carta tomorrow.

4. The first ten amendments to the constitution are usually referred to as the bill of rights.

5. This record of medieval music is very interesting.

6. Some of the most beautiful works of art were created during the renaissance.

7. The civil war is known officially as the war of the rebellion.

# 66

# Geographic Names

**The Rule**

The names of specific geographic locations such as rivers, mountains, and cities are capitalized.

Capitalize the name of each geographic location mentioned in the following sentences.

1. They are planning a trip to London, England next fall.

2. It seems that there is always some kind of trouble in at least one of the asian countries.

3. We saw hoover dam on our trip to the rocky mountains last summer.

4. My sister was surprised that the gulf of mexico looked just like the atlantic ocean off the coast of florida.

5. Last year we went to yellowstone park, and this year we plan to go to lake michigan.

6. They live in madison county, about a mile west of tylerville.

**67**

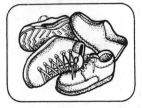

# Directional Terms

**The Rule** Directional words such as east and west, and the words that describe them are capitalized when they refer to a specific part of the country or world. (They are not capitalized when they simply refer to a direction.)

Capitalize the directional terms used as names and the words that are a part of the complete name.

1. Jack could not read enough about the Old West.

2. Do you think our next president is more likely to come from the northeast or from the southwest?

3. Now, this is hospitality like I remember from the deep south.

4. Which states are in the midwest?

5. What do you know about the most recent crisis in the middle east?

6. The Civil War was more complicated than just that the north and the south did not get along.

# 68

# Titles

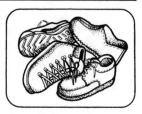

**The first and last word and the important words in between of titles of books, periodicals, poems, stories, chapters, articles, documents, movies, paintings and other works of art are capitalized.** *The Rule*

Capitalize the first and last and other important words in the titles mentioned in the following sentences.

1. Mindy likes to sit in front of the mirror and practice smiling like the **M**ona **L**isa.

2. Which did you enjoy more, the book titled **tom sawyer** or the movie version?

3. Janet's father likes to buy a copy of the Sunday edition of the **new york times**.

4. Do we really have to memorize the **declaration of independence?**

5. Randy wants a subscription to the **national geographic** for his birthday.

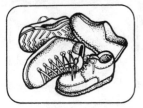

# Names of Time Periods

**The Rule** The names of months, days of the week, holidays, and special weeks are capitalized.

Capitalize the name of each month, day of the week, or holiday mentioned in the following sentences.

1. My brother always gets his Halloween costume ready the Saturday before he needs it.

2. december, january, and february are warm months in Chile.

3. Are passover and easter the same week this year?

4. The mailman does not deliver mail on sunday.

5. He works saturday and sunday but gets monday and tuesday off.

6. Do you plan to have turkey for thanksgiving?

7. Do you have any special activities planned for book week?

**70**

# Capitalizing in Sentences

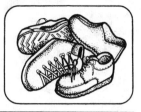

**The first word in every sentence and all proper nouns are capitalized.**

Capitalize the first word and all of the proper nouns in the following sentences.

1. We drove through the Blue Ridge Mountains on our way to Washington D. C.

2. janet has a dog named rover woolsey.

3. how far is it from new orleans, louisiana to little rock, arkansas?

4. the closest place to buy wilson's choco-lates is at the green parrot drugstore in johnson city.

5. we do not know whether to vote for ralph arthur or for sam rubenstein.

6. we crossed the missouri river in montana.

7. the first time he left new york, he went all the way to paris, france.

8. meet us at the american theater.

9. he joined the boy scouts.

10. they are canadians.

The Homework Booklet &copy;1983, Instructional Fair, Inc.

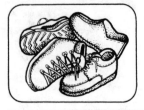

# Capitals in Poetry

**The Rule** The first word in each line of most traditional kinds of poems is capitalized.

Capitalize the first word in each of the lines of the following poem.

The Flag Goes By
by Henry Holcomb Bennett

Hats off!
along the street there comes
a blare of bugles, a ruffle of drums,
a flash of color beneath the sky:
hats off!
the flag is passing by!

blue and crimson and white it shines,
over the steel-tipped, ordered lines,
hats off!
the colors before us fly;
but more than the flag is passing by:

. . . .

sign of a nation, great and strong
to ward her people from foreign wrong:
pride and glory and honor—all
live in the colors to stand or fall.

. . . .

**72**

# Telling and Commanding Sentences

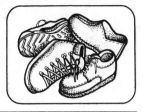

**A period (.) is placed at the end of each telling sentence and at the end of each sentence which gives a command.** The Rule

Put a period (.) at the end of each sentence in the following paragraph. If the sentence gives information or tells <u>how</u> to do something, circle the "t" (for telling); if the sentence gives a command or tells the reader <u>to</u> <u>do</u> something, circle the "c" (for command) after the sentence.

Many people like to prepare their own dried fruit. (t) c Sun drying is one of the easiest methods for drying fruit t c Just wash it, slice it, and lay it out in the sun t c Of course, anything dries fastest on bright, hot breezy days t c Use an electric fan to speed the drying process t c Test to be sure the fruit is dried t c Fruit is dry enough if no moisture comes out when it is squeezed t c

**73**

# Questions

**The Rule**  **A question mark (?) is placed at the end of each sentence which asks a question.**

How many teeth do you have?

Where does this go?

Decide which sentences in the following paragraph are questions, and change the punctuation of those sentences to a question mark (?). There are a total of three questions.

Do you think that ostriches bury their heads in the sand? The fact is that they do not. Their heads are very small compared to their bodies. Is it possible that people who watched an ostrich eating simply could not see its head. They might have thought the ostriches' heads were buried in the sand. We do know that a frightened baby ostrich drops its body to the ground and gets its head as low as possible. Is that the instinct that made ancient people think that an ostrich buries its head in the sand.

# 74

# Exclamatory Sentences

**An exclamation point (!) is placed at the end of each sentence which shows strong feeling.** *The Rule*

Stop doing that right now!

That dog might bite you!

Decide which sentences in the following paragraph show strong emotion and change the punctuation of those sentences to an exclamation point (!). There are a total of four.

You must hear what happened to me when I was in the jungle! First I was walking along a quiet path. All of a sudden, I heard a noise that frightened me right out of my skin. It turned out to be only a small bird with a very big voice. Then I saw a huge shadow shaped like a bull elephant ready to charge. But that turned out to be a tree with one big branch sticking out from the rest. The most frightening thing of all was when I slipped over the edge of a cliff. That is when I woke up.

**75**

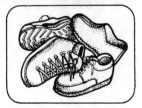

# City and State

**The Rule** **A comma (,) is placed between the name of a city and the state, district, or country, etc.**

St. Louis, Missouri   London, England

Put a comma (,) between the name of each city and state, district or country mentioned in the following sentences.

Ex. He moved to Seattle, Washington.

1. Major Pierre Charles L'Enfant drew the original plans for Washington District of Columbia.

2. The Mississippi begins near Lake Itaska Minnesota.

3. The Country Music Hall of Fame is located in Nashville Tennessee.

4. Buffalo Bill is buried on Lookout Mountain near Golden Colorado.

5. The Mission of San Miguel which is probably the oldest church in the United States is located in Santa Fe New Mexico.

# 76

# Day of Month and Year

**The Rule**

**A comma (,) is placed between the day of the month and the year. A comma (,) is also used after the year.**

He was born May 1, 1972, in Chicago.

Put a comma (,) between the name of each date and the year; put a comma (,) after the year mentioned in each of the sentences.

Ex. On December 7, 1787, Delaware became the first of the United States.

1. Alabama became a state on December 14 1819.

2. It was November 8   1889   that Montana became a state.

3. On June 1   1792   Kentucky became a state.

4. Alaska did not become a state until January 3   1959.

5. Idaho has been a state since July 3   1890.

6. Wyoming joined the Union on July 10 1890.

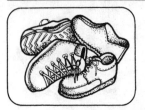

# Greetings and Closings

**The Rule** **A comma (,) is placed after the greeting in a friendly letter and after the closing of any letter.**

Dear Terry ,    Yours truly ,

Put a comma (,) after each greeting and closing of the letters below.

| | |
|---|---|
| Ex. | June 15, 1974 |
| Dear Terry, | |
| | Your friend ,<br>Jackie |

1.
Dear Anita

May 13, 1925

Sincerely
Margaret

2.
Dear Pedro

March 18, 1951

Yours truly
Jason

3.
Dear Mom

July 4, 1976

Your son
Aaron

**78**

# Punctuating Sentences

Place the correct punctuation mark on the blank at the end of each sentence in the following letter.

48 Reverberation Ave.
Sophistication, CA 94199
April 15, 1979

Dear Aunt Rhonda,

José and I can hardly wait until your visit! When will your bus arrive __ We have to know so we can meet you __

We thought we would miss the farm when we moved __ But we all really love this city __ __ We like being so close to the ocean, too __ __ By the way, how is everything on the farm __

The first thing we will do when you get unpacked is go to the beach __ __ Have you ever seen the ocean __ Don't forget your swimming suit __ __

Please hurry __

Your niece,
Maria

**79**

# Abbreviations

**The Rule**    An abbreviation is a short form of a word and is often followed by a period. Read the words in the box.

| | | | | | |
|---|---|---|---|---|---|
| Mon. | Tues. | Wed. | Thurs. | Fri. | Sat. |
| Sun. | Jan. | Feb. | Mar. | Apr. | Aug. |
| | Sept. | Oct. | Nov. | Dec. | |

1. Write the abbreviations for each day of the week.

   _____    _____    _____

   _____    _____    _____

   _____

2. Write the abbreviations of the names of the months that are abbreviated.

   _____    _____    _____

   _____    _____    _____

   _____    _____    _____

3. Write the words for these abbreviations.

   Feb. _____    Tues. _____

   Sept. _____    Wed. _____

**80**

# Abbreviations

Some words have short forms that are called abbreviations. You often put a period after an abbreviated word form. Write each abbreviation on the line next to the word for which it stands.

**The Rule**

| Word | | Abbreviations |
|------|---|---------------|
| 1. December | _____ | St. |
| 2. Friday | _____ | Dr. |
| 3. Mister | _____ | Sun. |
| 4. Street | _____ | Dec. |
| 5. United States | _____ | Ave. |
| 6 Sunday | _____ | Co. |
| 7. Doctor | _____ | U. S. |
| 8. Avenue | _____ | Aug. |
| 9. Company | _____ | Fri. |
| 10. August | _____ | Mr. |

## 81

# Abbreviations

abbreviation: shortened form of a word (or phrase) which stands for the whole word (or phrase).

Most abbreviations are used only in informal writing, such as notes, or when space is very limited.

**The Rule** **A period (.) is placed at the end of most common abbreviations.**

minute - <u>min</u>.   Mister - <u>Mr</u>.

Place a period (.) after each abbreviation in the following notes.

> Ex. Buy 3 lbs. of bacon at groc.

1. Be sure to watch Gov Michaels this eve   at 6  p m

2. field trip this Thurs

3. Aunt Betty's baby was born at 4:50 a m and weighed 7 lbs and 6 oz

4. need to buy 1 doz eggs and 1 pt of cream for angel food cake and icing

5. Vacation    starts    first    Mon in   Aug

# Initials

initial: first letter of a word or name; used in place of the word or name.

**A period (.) is placed after each initial. (Initials are usually capitalized).**

**cash on delivery = C.O.D.**

**District Attorney = D.A.**

Write the initials for each of the names or phrases listed below. Place a period (.) after each initial.

Ex. Rural Route <u>R.R.</u>

1. John Fitzgerald Kennedy _____

2. Parent Teacher Association _____

3. registered nurse _____

4. intelligence quotient _____

5. Federal Bureau of Investigation _____

6. Central Intelligence Agency _____

7. Boy Scouts of America _____

8. Franklin Delano Roosevelt _____

9. Theodore Roosevelt _____

## 83

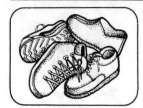

# Using the Dictionary

| cream | fasten | train | spread |
| black | produce | team | frost |
| deed | closely | solve | freedom |

Put the words in the box in alphabetical order.

1. _____     7. _____

2. _____     8. _____

3. _____     9. _____

4. _____     10. _____

5. _____     11. _____

6. _____     12. _____

Write the words from the box that would come between these sets of guide words.

13. __cart__ _____ _____

_____ debt _____

14. __soap__ _____ _____

_____ tame _____

# Dictionary Usage

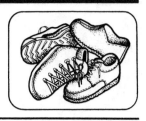

Each entry word in the dictionary is respelled. This respelling shows you how to say the entry word. **The Rule**

Draw a line from each entry word to its dictionary respelling. One is done for you.

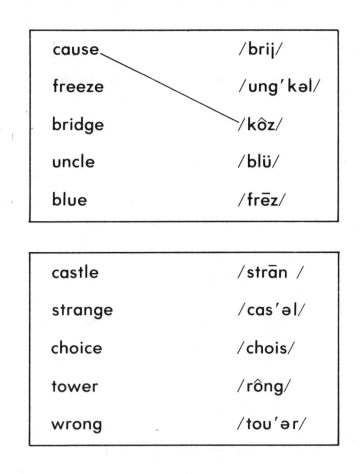

| cause | /brij/ |
| freeze | /ung'kəl/ |
| bridge | /kôz/ |
| uncle | /blü/ |
| blue | /frēz/ |

| castle | /strān / |
| strange | /cas'əl/ |
| choice | /chois/ |
| tower | /rông/ |
| wrong | /tou'ər/ |

# Using the Dictionary

Read the dictionary entries and the information following each entry.

chain (chān) 1. series of metal or other links joined together. 2. series of things joined as a mountain chain. 3. chains; pl. bonds, fetters.

bow (bō) 1. a device used to shoot arrows. 2. a device used to play a stringed instrument. 3. a decorative use of ribbon.

Write the number of the meaning of the underlined words in these sentences.

*Great job*

You have finished

this Book

1. ____ The state has a chain of low hills.

2. ____ Jan pulled the bow across the strings of his violin.

3. ____ The man was in chains.

4. ____ Tie a bow around the present.

## 86